SHOW ME HOW
I Can Make Music

Easy-to-make instruments for kids, shown step by step

MICHAEL PURTON

ARMADILLO

To Sue, Alice, Helen and John Purton,
with thanks for all their help

This edition is published by Armadillo,
an imprint of Anness Publishing Ltd, 108 Great Russell Street,
London WC1B 3NA; info@anness.com

www.annesspublishing.com

If you like the images in this book and would like to
investigate using them for publishing, promotions or
advertising, please visit our website www.practicalpictures.com
for more information.

Publisher: Joanna Lorenz
Project Editors: Judith Simons and Richard McGinlay
Designer: Edward Kinsey
Photographers: John Freeman, with James Duncan
Stylist: Thomasina Smith
Production Controller: Rosie Anness

We would like to thank the following children who were such
wonderful models, and their parents: Benjamin Ferguson,
Lorenzo Green, Nicholas Lie, Gabriella and Izabella
Malewska, Ilaira and Joshua Mallalieu, Jessica and Alice
Moxley, Alice Purton and Claudius Wilson.

PUBLISHER'S NOTE
The level of adult supervision needed will depend on the age
and ability of the children following the projects. However, we
advise that adult supervision is always preferable and vital if
the project calls for the use of sharp knives or other objects.
See the exclamation mark symbol for more information on
where adult help is needed.

Although the advice and information in this book are
believed to be accurate and true at the time of going to press,
neither the author nor the publisher can accept any legal
responsibility or liability for any errors or omissions that may
have been made nor for any inaccuracies nor for any loss,
harm or injury that comes about from following instructions
or advice in this book.

Manufacturer: Anness Publishing Ltd,
108 Great Russell Street, London WC1B 3NA, England
For Product Tracking go to:
www.annesspublishing.com/tracking
Batch: 1418-22721-1127

Contents

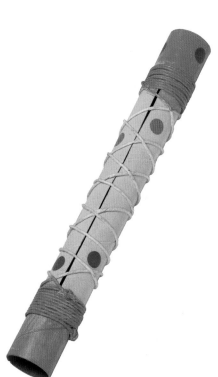

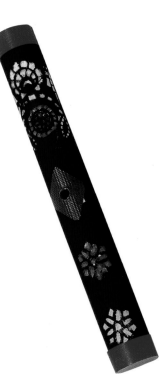

Introduction

What is music? Very simply, music is made from sounds that are pleasing or interesting to hear. Birdsong can be described as music and so can the sounds of the wind or the sea. Many people who write music – composers – have copied the sounds of nature in their music.

Sound is caused by vibrations in the air. The stronger the vibrations, the louder the sound. Musical instruments help us to make music by producing many different sounds. Your own voice is a musical instrument. See how many sounds you can make by altering the shape of your mouth, changing the pitch of your voice from high to low, and using your tongue in different ways. We humans are a mixture of the different types of instruments described below: we are wind instruments because we use air to make sounds; stringed instruments because we speak or sing through our vocal cords, which are like strings low down in our throats; and percussion instruments because we can clap our hands and snap our fingers.

Gabriella's bottle xylophone is a percussion instrument.

Musicians divide musical instruments into different groups:

Percussion instruments

These are all the instruments that you hit. They were probably the earliest instruments. People from long ago made music by hitting bones together, or hitting a hollow tree. Animal skins were stretched over pots or bits of tree trunks to make drums. It is not just drums that are percussion instruments. There are all kinds of fun shakers and rattles which are also used to give rhythm in music.

Wind instruments

These are the instruments that you blow. The air vibrates inside the hollow instrument and makes a sound. The first instruments of this kind were made out of hollow animal horns or bones. Wind instruments sometimes have a "reed" to help make a good sound, and a drinking straw works very well for this.

Stringed instruments

These instruments can be plucked with your fingers or played with a bow. The strings were first made out of hair and silk. All stringed instruments need a hollow box of some kind over which the strings are attached. The box is full of air, which vibrates when you play the instrument.

Claudius has made a bugle, which is a wind instrument.

This shoebox guitar is a stringed instrument. The strings are made from rubber bands.

Jessica is making a drum from a mini plastic wastebasket.

Musical families

See how many instruments you can think of and try to place them in a family or group. Is the piano a stringed instrument? It has strings but they are not plucked or played with a bow. If you look inside the piano you will see that small felt hammers hit the strings to make the sounds. It is a percussion instrument!

Making musical instruments

This chapter will help you to discover lots of different sounds by making your own instruments and then playing them. They are very easy to make. All you need to make music is a cardboard tube or drinks can, and a few bottle caps or a bath hat! Some of the instruments come from countries like Africa and Latin America, so it is a good chance to decorate them with really bright shades. If you make one of the fun shakers or rattles, it will feel like carnival time!

It is great fun to make music with someone else to help.

Maracas are filled with rice or beans and make a wonderful sound when shaken in the air.

Making music together

It is even more fun playing music in groups. Perhaps you and your friends can each make a different instrument to play. First try a rhythm game. Each of you choose a word and then play the rhythm (the beat) of that word on your instruments over and over again. Try to keep time with everyone else, then experiment by getting louder then softer, and slower then faster.

You could join in with pop song that you like. Start with the percussion instruments to make the rhythm, then add a wind instrument like a kazoo to sing the tune. See how many different instruments you can use. Make up some music to describe a storm, a ghost story, or a trip to the zoo.

This reed pipe is a very simple kind of oboe made from a cardboard tube with a drinking straw for the "reed".

Equipment and materials

All the musical instruments in this book are easy to make at home. There are some basic pieces of equipment and some craft materials that you will need to make and decorate the projects, such as paper, glue, paints, paintbrushes, scissors and felt-tipped pens. If you look after your equipment and tidy all the pieces away when you have finished at the end of the day, they will last a long time and you will be able to use them again and again.

Paper and cardboard These are available in a variety of shades, making them fun and quick to use. But you can use white cardboard and paper instead and decorate them using paints, stickers or felt-tipped pens.

Stickers and string You can get bright and shiny stickers in lots of shades, shapes and sizes and use them to liven up your musical instruments. Bright string can also be used to decorate your instruments.

Paints and paintbrushes There are many different kinds of paint, but the easiest to use are acrylic paints or poster paints. You can mix them with water to make them runny, or use them thick if you want a very bright shade. If you are using more than one shade, have several brushes to work with – one for each. Rinse your brushes under running water as soon as you have finished, otherwise the paint will go hard and you will spoil the brushes.

Paint pots These are pots with special lids which stop the paint spilling if you knock them over by mistake. They are very useful if you want to mix up a lot of paint and save some to use later. Wash out the pots with clean water before you put a different shade of paint in them.

Felt-tipped pens These are great to use for decorating. Some are water-based and wash off your hands and clothes easily. The inks cannot be mixed like paints, so it is best to use them separately.

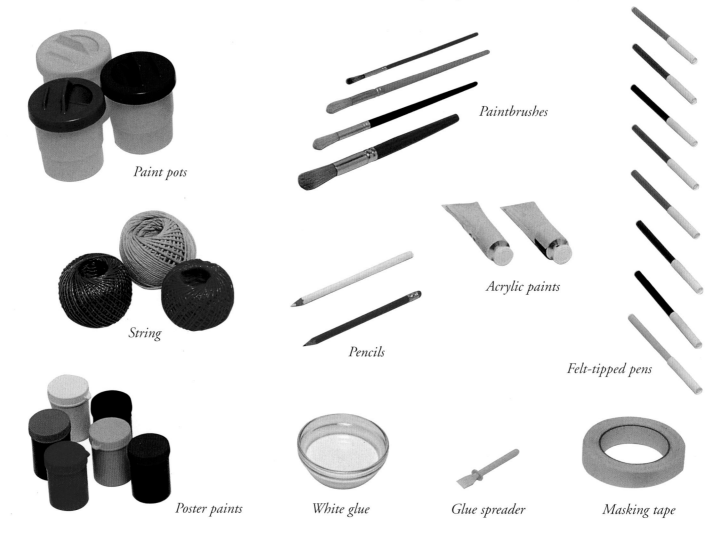

Paint pots

Paintbrushes

String

Pencils

Acrylic paints

Felt-tipped pens

Poster paints

White glue

Glue spreader

Masking tape

Glues White glue is the best glue to use because it will wash off your hands and brushes. It is white to begin with, as its name suggests, but when it dries it becomes invisible. It is also known as PVA glue. You can apply it using a glue brush or a glue spreader. It will stick most things together – wood, paper, cardboard, fabric and plastic. Papier-mâché is made from newspaper mixed with white glue and water (3 parts glue to 1 part water). White glue is very strong when it is dry. Glue sticks are easy to use for sticking paper.

Adhesive tapes There are various different kinds. Masking tape is very useful because it does not stick permanently, like other kinds of plastic tape. You can use it to hold things together while glue dries, and then remove it easily. Clear adhesive tape can also be used if you want to stick things together for good. You can get adhesive tapes in lots of bright shades for decorating your musical instruments. Electrical or insulating tape, which electricians use, is ideal and comes in different widths as well as shades.

Scissors and craft knives Always be very careful when you are using scissors. Use ones which have rounded ends whenever you can. If you need to use pointed scissors or a craft knife to pierce cans or cut out circles, for example, ALWAYS ask a grown-up to do this for you.

Pencil, ruler and eraser Always use a ruler if you need to measure anything and draw straight lines. Use a sharp pencil with a soft lead to make marks that you do not want to show and rub them out later.

Apron Always wear an apron or an old shirt over your clothes in case you make a mess. Then you will have something to wipe your fingers on!

Cloth It is always a good idea to have a cloth handy when you are using paints and glues, just in case you have an accident and need to clean it up quickly.

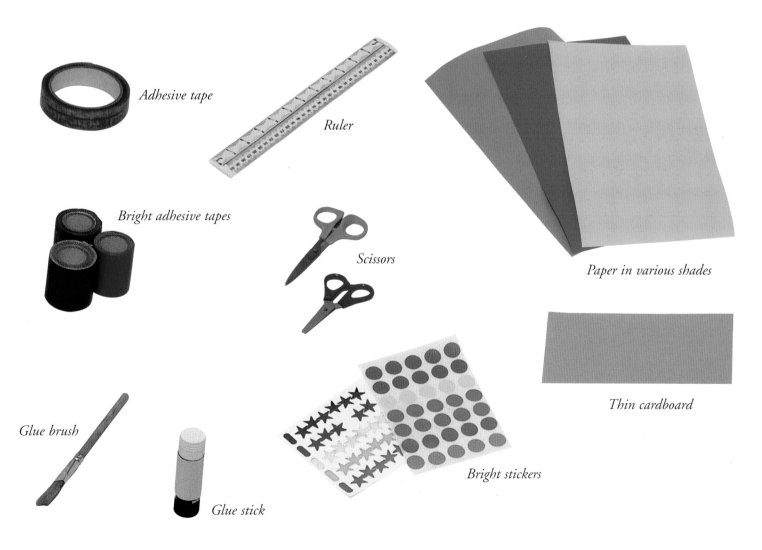

Adhesive tape

Ruler

Bright adhesive tapes

Scissors

Paper in various shades

Thin cardboard

Glue brush

Glue stick

Bright stickers

9

Materials from Around the Home

All the musical instruments in this book are made using materials and equipment you will find at home. Ordinary objects like metal pan lids, cardboard boxes and drinks cans make wonderful sounds if you know what to do with them. Look out for packaging and containers which you can use for making music. Cardboard tubes are really useful – collect long ones from wrapping paper, medium-sized ones from kitchen paper or foil, and small ones from toilet rolls. Ask a grown-up for spare bits of knitting wool, ribbon, cord and beads from the sewing box, and garden hose and flowerpots from the garden shed.

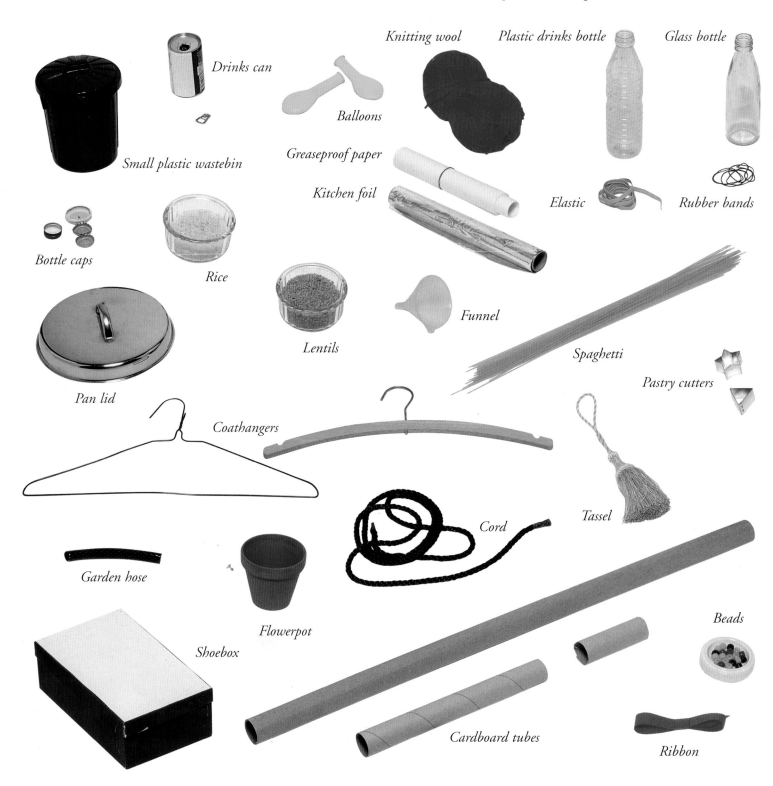

Drinks can

Knitting wool

Plastic drinks bottle

Glass bottle

Balloons

Small plastic wastebin

Greaseproof paper

Kitchen foil

Elastic

Rubber bands

Bottle caps

Rice

Lentils

Funnel

Spaghetti

Pastry cutters

Pan lid

Coathangers

Tassel

Cord

Garden hose

Flowerpot

Beads

Shoebox

Cardboard tubes

Ribbon

Cutting Out a Circle

It can be difficult to cut a circle out of cardboard. The best way to do it is to ask a grown-up to stab a small hole in the middle of the circle, using the point of a sharp pair of scissors. Then make several small cuts outwards to the edge of the circle. You will now be able to cut around the edge of the circle quite easily.

Cut out towards the edge of the circle.

Then carefully cut around the circle itself.

Painting Straight Lines

Masking tape is very useful for this. Stick the tape along the line, then paint right up to it. You can paint a little over the edge. Wait for the paint to dry completely, then pull off the tape and you will have a perfectly straight line. This is a good way to paint shapes like triangles and diamonds.

Use masking tape to help paint straight lines.

Painting Plastic

To make paint stick to plastic surfaces, add the same amount of white glue as the amount of paint and stir well. If the mixture is too thick, add a little water.

Varnishing

White glue can also be used to make varnish, which will protect the surface of your musical instruments. Mix the glue with twice the amount of water. The varnish will look a bit white when you paint it on, but when it dries it will be clear.

Mix white glue with water to make a varnish.

Using Tape

Applying adhesive tape can be tricky and it is quite easy to get all tangled up! Here are some ideas to help you.

If you are covering something in tape, do not cut it first. Wait until you have finished and then cut it.

If you only need a small piece of tape, make a small cut with the scissors. Now grip the tape firmly with both hands and tear a piece off.

⚠ A Note for Grown-ups

Most of the musical instruments in this book can be made by a child alone, with a little bit of adult help. However, always supervise your children closely whenever they are using craft materials. The places in the book where your assistance is vital, such as when sharp scissors or a craft knife are needed, are marked with the symbol shown above.

Clashing Castanets

❗Children may need help measuring out and cutting and scoring the cardboard.

Castanets come from Spain, where they are used in flamenco dancing. The dancers stamp their feet and click their castanets in time to the music. It is very exciting to watch them. See if you can dance the same way. Izabella has made her castanets with metal pastry-cutters, so they make a wonderful sound. *Olé!*

YOU WILL NEED THESE MATERIALS AND TOOLS

White cardboard

Pencil

Ruler

Scissors

Poster paints, in two shades

Paintbrushes

Thin cardboard, in the shade of your choice

White glue and brush

4 small pastry (cookie) cutters

Black felt-tipped pen

Bright adhesive tape

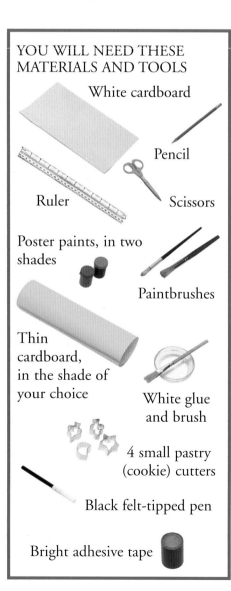

Put your thumb and middle finger through the yellow finger-holders and play away!

1 Draw a rectangle 20cm (8in) long and 7cm (3in) wide on white cardboard. Draw two lines 4cm (1½in) apart down the middle of the rectangle.

2 Carefully cut out the rectangle. Bend the cardboard along the middle lines. It helps if you score along the lines with the ruler first.

3 Paint one side of the cardboard. Leave to dry, then paint the other side in a different shade. Leave to dry while you make the finger-holders.

4 Draw four small rectangles on thin cardboard and cut out. Fold around into tubes to fit your middle finger and thumb, and glue together.

5 Decorate one side of the painted cardboard. Draw around the pastry cutters with a black felt-tipped pen to make outline shapes.

6 Reinforce the middle where the castanets bend with some bright adhesive tape. This will make them last for longer.

7 Glue the finger-holders onto the decorated side of the cardboard. Place them about 1cm (½in) each side of the bend. Leave to dry.

8 Glue a pastry cutter to the inside ends of each castanet. Use plenty of glue and let it dry properly. Then you can play your castanets!

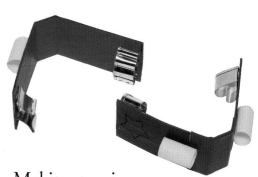

Making music

Clash the pastry cutters together in time to the music. You can also play them by resting your hand on a table.

Dustbin Drum

Drums are very old instruments. They are used for the rhythm in dance music and they help soldiers to keep in step when they march. Drums were also once used to send signals because you can hear them so far away. You can play your drum with bare hands or with beaters, like Jessica and Alice.

Making music

Do not hit the drum too hard. You will get the best sound if you hit it close to the edge. If you hit different parts of the drumskin, you will get different sounds. Try playing it with a pair of chopsticks or your hands.

! A grown-up should cut the cork in half with a craft knife and push the skewer into the corks, to make the beaters. Children may need help with scissors.

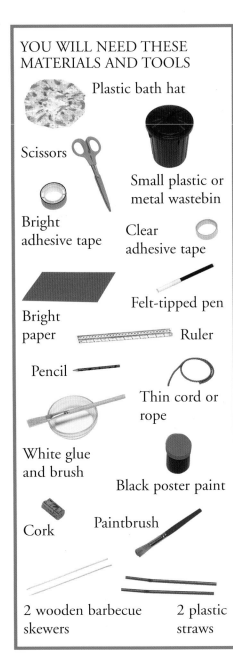

YOU WILL NEED THESE
MATERIALS AND TOOLS

Plastic bath hat

Scissors

Small plastic or metal wastebin

Bright adhesive tape

Clear adhesive tape

Bright paper

Felt-tipped pen

Pencil

Ruler

Thin cord or rope

White glue and brush

Black poster paint

Cork

Paintbrush

2 wooden barbecue skewers

2 plastic straws

The finished drum looks very smart.

1 Cut the elastic out of the bath hat. Draw around a plate that is 5cm (2in) bigger all around than the top of the wastebin. Cut the circle out.

2 Decorate the bin with stripes of bright adhesive tape.

3 Stretch the plastic circle tightly over the open end of the bin. Stick it in place with several small tabs of adhesive tape.

4 Make sure the plastic drumskin is really tight, then tape right around the edge to hold it in place.

5 Cut a strip of paper to fit around the bin top. Make small cuts on both sides for a fringe.

6 Glue the fringe around the top of the bin.

7 Tie the cord or rope around the middle of the fringe.

8 Ask a grown-up to cut the cork in half across the middle. Paint the corks black. Push the skewers through the straws, then ask a grown-up to push them into the corks.

Guiro Scraper

In Latin America, guiros are often made out of dried gourds with notches cut in the side. Gourds are a type of large fruit with a hard shell. The musicians scrape the notches with a stick to make a harsh noise. Sometimes the sound is like the call of a woodpecker or jungle bird. Alice has painted her tube in bright shades like a real guiro player.

Guiros are used to provide rhythm in Latin American dance music.

Making music

Scrape the stick backwards and forwards across the slit. The string will vibrate and make a noise. A guiro made from a hard material, like thick bamboo, will make a louder sound. Ask a grown-up to cut a long slit along the bamboo pole to help the vibrating air escape, and some small notches across the pole.

! Children will need help cutting the slit in the cardboard tube.

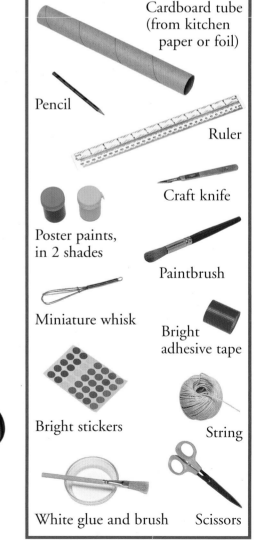

YOU WILL NEED THESE MATERIALS AND TOOLS

Cardboard tube (from kitchen paper or foil)

Pencil

Ruler

Craft knife

Poster paints, in 2 shades

Paintbrush

Miniature whisk

Bright adhesive tape

Bright stickers

String

White glue and brush

Scissors

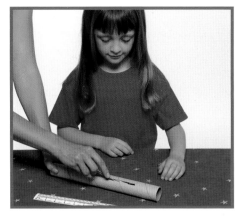

1 Draw a line about 20cm (8in) down the side of the cardboard tube. Ask a grown-up to cut a slit along the line with a craft knife.

2 Paint the whole tube in one shade. Put it on one side to dry while you make the rhythm stick.

3 Decorate the end of the whisk with bright adhesive tape. Wind it around several times as this will make it comfortable to hold.

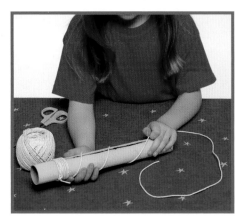

4 Cut a piece of string 2m (6ft) long. Tie it tightly to the tube 5cm (2in) above the slit. Wind the string around the tube up to the slit, then wind it diagonally across the slit.

5 Wind the string around the other end of the tube, then wind it diagonally back across the slit to make a criss-cross pattern. Fasten tightly with a knot. Decorate between the string with stickers.

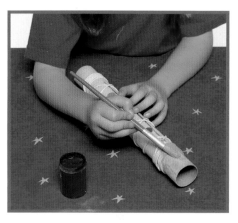

6 Paint the ends of the tube a different shade. Mix the paint with the same amount of glue and a little water to make it stick.

7 Paint the rest of the tube with glue. The glue will hold the string and the stickers in place.

Deep Box Bass

Bass instruments play the very lowest notes. This is because they are so large. The large box and the large hole mean there is plenty of space for the air to vibrate and make a deep, booming sound. Nicholas is plucking his box bass with his fingers, like a double-bass player in a jazz band.

Your box bass is all ready for a jazz session!

Making music

Hold the elastic with one hand and twang it with the other. You can change the sound by pressing the elastic in different places. Thick elastic makes a lower sound than thin elastic.

A grown-up should cut the cork in half with a craft knife. Children may need help with scissors.

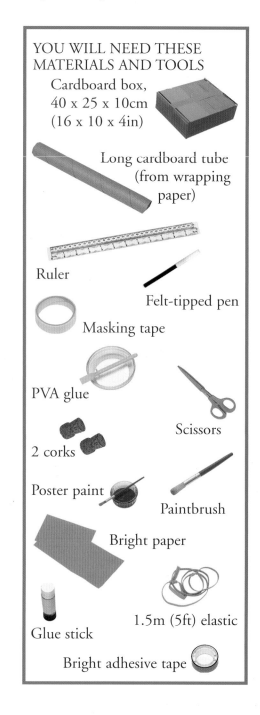

YOU WILL NEED THESE MATERIALS AND TOOLS

Cardboard box, 40 x 25 x 10cm (16 x 10 x 4in)

Long cardboard tube (from wrapping paper)

Ruler

Felt-tipped pen

Masking tape

PVA glue

Scissors

2 corks

Poster paint

Paintbrush

Bright paper

Glue stick

1.5m (5ft) elastic

Bright adhesive tape

1 Draw around the cardboard tube to make a circle on the middle of the box top. Then draw around the roll of masking tape to make a larger circle on the box front. Position it as shown.

2 Carefully cut out both circles. Pierce the circle with the scissors, and make small cuts out towards the edge of the circle. Then cut all around the edge of the circle.

3 Push the tube through the small hole. Glue and tape the tube in place. Ask a grown-up to cut a cork in half. Glue and tape one half as shown and the other below the large hole.

4 Paint the box and the tube, and leave to dry.

5 Draw musical notes on the paper. Draw around a cork to make the circle shapes.

6 Cut out the notes and glue them onto the front of the box.

7 Ask a grown-up to cut an 8cm (3in) slit in the front of the tube. Tie the elastic around the bottom. Tie a double knot in the other end.

8 Decorate the box with tape. Stretch the elastic down the back of the box and back up the front. Slip the knot into the slit in the tube.

The Projects

Singing Kazoo

This is a very unusual instrument. You sing through it and it makes your voice sound very strange. Indian musicians play a kind of kazoo which they hold against their throats when they sing. Lorenzo has covered his kazoo with stencils. This is a very easy and quick way to decorate things.

Making music
Sing through the hole in the middle of the kazoo. You can play any tune you like. Experiment with a smaller cardboard tube, such as from a toilet roll, and see if it sounds different.

!️ A grown-up should make the hole in the cardboard tube and in the adhesive tape. Children may need help with scissors.

YOU WILL NEED THESE MATERIALS AND TOOLS

Cardboard tube (from kitchen paper or foil)

Scissors

Paintbrushes

Poster paint, in white and two other shades

Paper doily

Masking tape

Baking parchment

Felt-tipped pen

White glue and brush

40cm (16in) paper ribbon

Bright adhesive tape

20

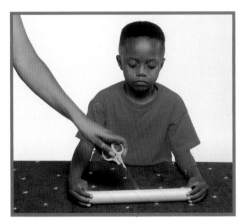

1 Ask a grown-up to make a small hole in the middle of the cardboard tube.

2 Use the end of a paintbrush to smooth the edges of the hole.

3 Paint the cardboard tube. Leave the paint to dry.

4 Cut flower shapes from the paper doily and use them as stencils. Stick them onto the tube with masking tape and paint over them. Leave the paint to dry, then remove the stencils.

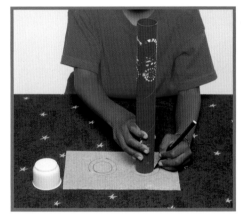

5 Draw two circles on the baking parchment. Draw around a cup or any round object that is slightly larger than the end of the tube. Now draw around the end of the tube to make a smaller circle inside each larger one.

6 Cut out the large circles. Make small cuts between the large and small circles. This will give each circle a frill around the edge. Brush glue onto the frills.

7 Stretch the baking parchment circles tightly across the ends of the cardboard tube. Press the frills around the sides of the tube.

8 Glue ribbon around the ends of the tube. Stick a piece of bright adhesive tape over the hole. Ask a grown-up to pierce through the tape.

Stencils are a good way to decorate any of the instruments in this book.

Twirling Japanese Drum

Different parts of the world have different kinds of music and different instruments. Lorenzo's little Japanese drum has a handle so that he can twirl it between his fingers. It makes a lovely rattling sound. When the drum is moving fast, the paper swirls look as if they are spinning around.

You could add extra strings and more beads to your drum if you like.

Making music
Hold the handle of the drum between your palms and twirl it backwards and forwards. The beads will fly up and hit the drum.

! A grown-up should make the holes in the side of the box lid and base. Children may need help with scissors.

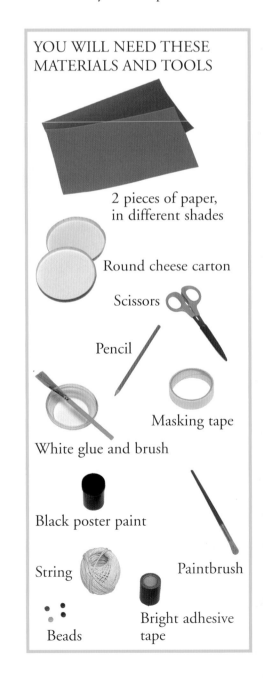

YOU WILL NEED THESE MATERIALS AND TOOLS

2 pieces of paper, in different shades

Round cheese carton

Scissors

Pencil

Masking tape

White glue and brush

Black poster paint

String

Paintbrush

Beads

Bright adhesive tape

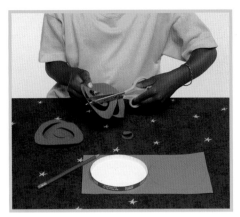

1 Draw twice around the carton lid on one piece of paper. Cut out the circles. Cut them into swirls. Cut two circles from the other piece of paper.

2 Ask a grown-up to make a hole in the side of the box lid and one in the side of the base, large enough to push the pencil through. Put on the lid.

3 Push the pencil through the holes and secure it with glue and masking tape. Tape around the side of the box and paint the tape black.

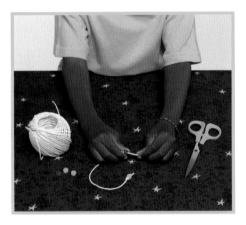

4 Cut a piece of string about 30cm (12in) long. Tie a double knot at one end. Thread one or two beads onto the string, then tie another knot. Repeat at the other end of the string.

5 Spread glue over one side of the box. Lay the string carefully across the middle so that it is central, with the same amount of string showing on each side.

6 Cover the glue and string with one of the whole circles of paper. Glue one of the paper swirls on top. Glue a paper circle and a swirl to the other side of the box. Leave to dry.

7 Decorate the pencil handle with bright adhesive tape. Leave some of the pencil showing to make stripes.

Metal Wind Chimes

You do not have to play these wind chimes yourself – if you hang them up, the wind will play them for you. The best place to hang them is from a door frame or window frame. If there is a breeze, the chimes make a tinkling sound. Benjamin likes to play his chimes himself, using a metal spoon.

Ask a grown-up for an old metal spoon which you can keep to play your wind chimes. Decorate it with bright stickers.

Making music
Run a metal spoon along the chimes and back again. Or you can strike each object separately.

! A grown-up should remove the ring pulls from the drinks cans and cover any sharp edges with thick adhesive tape. A grown-up should also pierce the bottle caps and drinks cans using a corkscrew or some other sharp object.

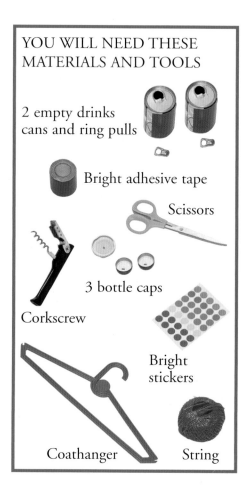

YOU WILL NEED THESE MATERIALS AND TOOLS

2 empty drinks cans and ring pulls

Bright adhesive tape

Scissors

3 bottle caps

Corkscrew

Bright stickers

Coathanger   String

1 Wash the drinks cans and leave to dry. Cover them with bright adhesive tape.

2 Ask a grown-up to make a hole in each of the bottle caps, using the corkscrew or a similar sharp object.

3 Ask the grown-up to also make a hole in the bottoms of the drinks cans for you.

4 Decorate the cans and the bottle caps with lots of bright stickers.

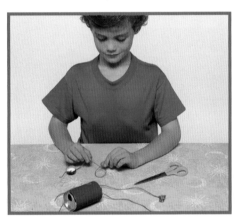

5 Thread the cans, ring pulls and bottle tops onto pieces of string. Knot the string to keep them in place.

6 Tie all the pieces of string onto the coathanger.

Experiment with different chimes. Try small pieces of copper pipe. You could also use bamboo or strips of kitchen foil.

Shoebox Guitar

The guitar is probably the most popular instrument of all. It is easy to carry and you can play many different kinds of music on it. Jessica is plucking the elastic string on her guitar, just like a pop star. Electric guitars don't have boxes full of air like this one, so they need electricity to make them sound loud.

Making music

Pluck the elastic string with one hand. With your other hand, press the elastic against the cardboard tube. If you press in different places, you can change the note. Try strumming the string with a coin instead of plucking it.

! Children may need help cutting out the circles. See the Introduction for an easy way of doing this.

A guitar is a large box full of air. The air vibrates and makes the sound, which escapes through the hole.

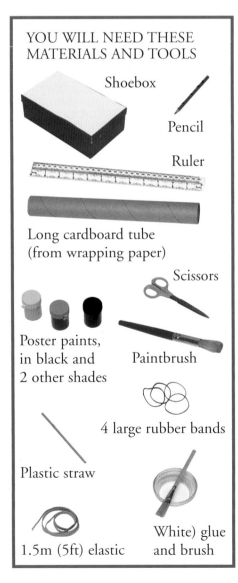

YOU WILL NEED THESE MATERIALS AND TOOLS

Shoebox

Pencil

Ruler

Long cardboard tube (from wrapping paper)

Scissors

Poster paints, in black and 2 other shades

Paintbrush

4 large rubber bands

Plastic straw

White) glue and brush

1.5m (5ft) elastic

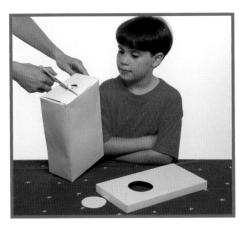

1 Draw a 10cm (4in) circle on the box lid. Draw around the tube on one end of the box base. Ask a grown-up to cut out the circles.

2 Draw a guitar shape on the lid of the box. Use a circular shape as a guide, or use a pair of compasses, if you like.

3 Outline the guitar shape in black paint. Fill in with another shade of paint, then paint the rest of the box with a third shade. Paint the tube.

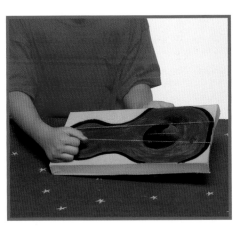

4 Stretch two rubber bands across the lid. Position them as shown, just on the edge of the hole.

5 Put the lid on the box. Hold it in place with two more rubber bands. Cut the straw in half. Slide the two pieces under the rubber bands at each end of the guitar. Glue in place.

6 Cut a slit about 8cm (3in) long at one end of the tube. Tie a knot in one end of the elastic. Make a loop in the other end and slide it over the end of the tube.

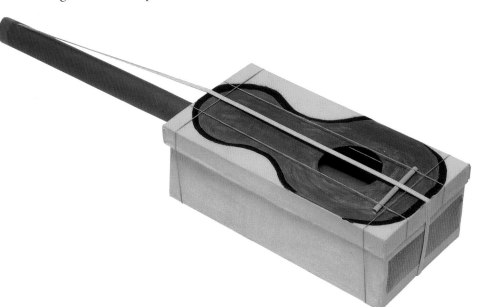

7 Push the tube into the hole in the box. Stretch the elastic around the back of the box and up around the front. Slip the knot into the slit in the tube.

Multiple Instrument

Not sure whether to make a double bass, a scraper or a drum? If so, then this is the instrument for you! You can pluck or bow the string, run a stick over the corrugated paper, and you can even hit the top or sides like a drum.

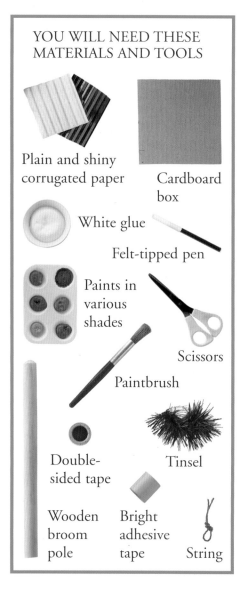

YOU WILL NEED THESE MATERIALS AND TOOLS

Plain and shiny corrugated paper

Cardboard box

White glue

Felt-tipped pen

Paints in various shades

Scissors

Paintbrush

Double-sided tape

Tinsel

Wooden broom pole

Bright adhesive tape

String

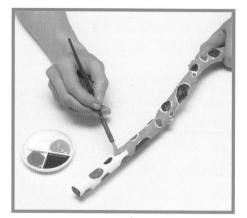

Rhythm sticks

Thin pieces of branch make great percussion sticks, so look out for them the next time you are out in a park or wood. Make sure the branches are dry, so that they make a loud noise when you use them. Decorate them using poster paints. If you wish, seal the surface with non-toxic craft varnish after the paint has dried.

1 Stick a piece of corrugated paper around the upright sides of the cardboard box with white glue, making sure it is smooth.

2 Using a felt-tipped pen, draw a circle on one side of the box and carefully cut it out with scissors to make a hole.

3 Glue a piece of shiny corrugated paper on the top of the box. Paint the rest of the box using a bright shade of paint.

4 Stick the tinsel around the hole using either glue or some double-sided tape.

5 Paint the wooden broom pole and attach it to the side of the box using bright adhesive tape.

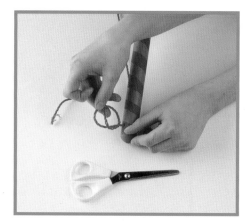

6 Thread the string through the hole at the top of the pole and tie a knot. Make a hole at the top and bottom of the box and thread the string through. Tie a knot to secure. It will need to be very tight to make a noise.

Caxixi Rattle

The name of this rattle is pronounced "casheeshee". It comes from Latin America. You can fill it with anything that will make a good sound – try rice or beans, or sand. Alice has made a face for her rattle with scraps of paper and stickers. She has also given it a wonderful fringe.

! A grown-up should puncture the bottle and children may need help with scissors.

Shake your caxixi rattle in time to your favourite music.

Making music

Make two caxixi rattles and shake them together. Try this until you can keep in time to the rhythm of the music. Fill the bottles with different things to make different sounds.

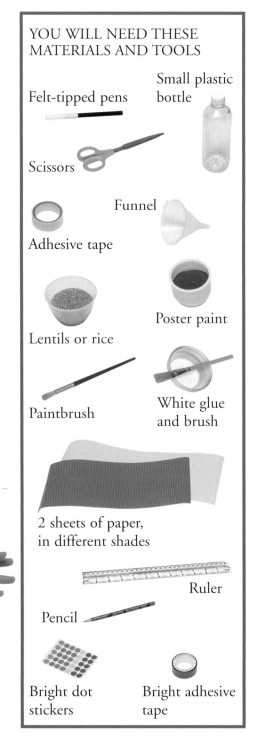

YOU WILL NEED THESE MATERIALS AND TOOLS

Felt-tipped pens

Small plastic bottle

Scissors

Funnel

Adhesive tape

Poster paint

Lentils or rice

Paintbrush

White glue and brush

2 sheets of paper, in different shades

Ruler

Pencil

Bright dot stickers

Bright adhesive tape

1 Wash and dry the bottle. Draw a line around the bottle about one-third from the top. Draw another line the same distance from the bottom.

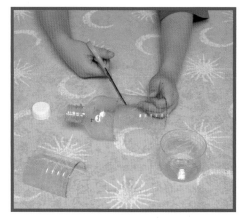

2 Ask a grown-up to puncture the bottle with the point of the scissors. Then cut along both the lines you have marked.

3 Stick the top and bottom pieces of the bottle together with adhesive tape to make a shorter bottle shape. Pour the lentils or rice into the bottle.

4 Mix the paint with glue and a little water and paint the top half of the bottle. Leave to dry.

5 Cut a strip from each of the sheets of paper, long enough to wrap around the bottle.

6 To make a fringe, fold the strips over and make plenty of small cuts halfway across the strips of paper.

7 Glue the fringe around the bottle. Hold it in place with bright tape. Decorate your caxixi with a funny face using the dot stickers, the paper and the felt-tipped pen.

This is a different caxixi shape made from a drinks can and then decorated with star stickers and adhesive tape.

Tambourine Flower

Tambourines have been played since the Middle Ages. They were made of a circle of wood with very thin animal skin stretched across, and they had bells around the edge. Like castanets, tambourines are very popular in Spanish dancing – you could play them together. Leslie has painted his tambourine to look like a sunflower.

Instead of bottle caps, you could use beads or buttons. They will all make different sounds.

Making music

Hold your tambourine above your head and shake it. You can also hold it in one hand and tap it with the fingers of your other hand. You can even bang it against your knee.

⚠️ A grown-up should pierce the bottle caps using a corkscrew or other sharp object. Children may need help with scissors.

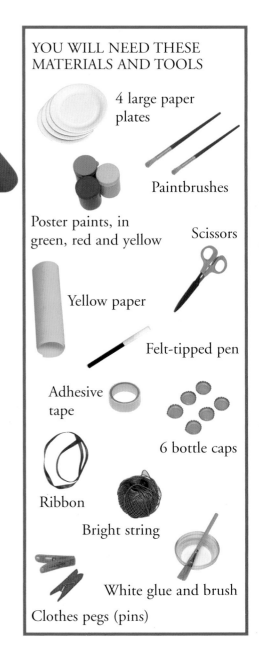

YOU WILL NEED THESE MATERIALS AND TOOLS

4 large paper plates

Paintbrushes

Poster paints, in green, red and yellow

Scissors

Yellow paper

Felt-tipped pen

Adhesive tape

6 bottle caps

Ribbon

Bright string

White glue and brush

Clothes pegs (pins)

1 Using green paint, paint around the rim of one of the paper plates. Do not paint the middle. Leave the paint to dry.

2 Cut a long strip of yellow paper. Fold the strip over and over. Draw a petal shape on the top layer and cut out through all the layers. Repeat to make 16 petals.

3 Tape the petal shapes around the unpainted circle in the middle of the plate.

4 Take another paper plate. Cut out the middle circle and paint it in red. Leave to dry.

5 Paint spots of yellow on the red circle. Paint the bottle caps red as well. Leave to dry.

6 Cut the ribbon into several pieces, each roughly the same length. Cut two pieces of string the same length and knot at one end. Ask a grown-up to pierce the bottle caps. Thread three onto each piece of string, tying a knot after each one.

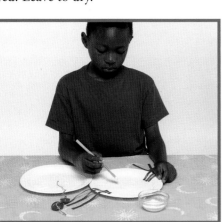

7 Take the third paper plate. Glue three or four ribbons on each side. Glue the string on each side of the fourth plate. Glue the plates together.

8 Put clothes pegs round the edge, to make sure the plates stick together properly. Leave the glue to dry.

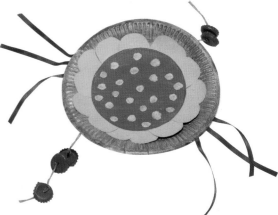

Pan-lid Cymbals

These pan lids make terrific cymbals. You can hit one with a beater, or clash them together as Benjamin is doing. Be careful not to bang them directly together – to do a proper cymbal clash, you move one cymbal up and one down. Real cymbals can turn inside out if you hit them directly together! Cymbals are often played with drums in a drum kit.

Making music

Cymbals are often played very loudly, but they can also make a lovely, quiet sound. You can also hold a cymbal by its handle, or hang is from a piece of string, and strike it with one of your homemade beaters.

! A grown-up should cut the cork in half using a craft knife. Children will need help pushing the skewer into the cork.

YOU WILL NEED THESE MATERIALS AND TOOLS

2 matching metal pan lids

Bright stickers

Ribbon

Scissors

Narrow and wide bright adhesive tape

Large bottle-washer

Wooden barbecue skewer

Cork

Pan scourer

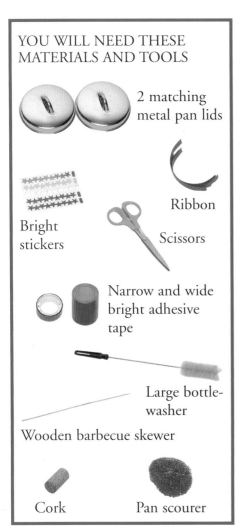

If you want to decorate your pan-lid cymbals, check with a grown-up first to make sure they don't mind!

1 Decorate the pan lids with stickers. Arrange them in a circle, following the shape of the lid. Decorate the ribbon with stickers.

2 Decorate the handles with several strips of ribbon. Loop the strips around the handle and stick together with narrow adhesive tape.

3 Cover the rest of the handles with wide adhesive tape. Wind the narrow adhesive tape around the handle to make stripes.

4 Now make the first stick. Decorate the handle of the bottle-washer with stickers and adhesive tape.

5 Make the second stick. Push the wooden skewer through the middle of the pan scourer. Ask a grown-up to cut the cork in half. Push the sharp end of the skewer into one piece of cork.

6 Wind adhesive tape around the cork and the skewer where it comes out below the pan scourer. This will stop the pan scourer from slipping down the handle.

The two beaters make very different sounds.

The Projects

Snakey Maracas

Maracas are played by shaking them in time to the music. The rice inside rattles around to make the sound. Maracas are very popular in Africa and Latin America, where they are often made out of gourds.
Nicholas has made his maracas out of papier-mâché. This is wet newspaper mixed with glue. When it is dry, it sets hard so that you can paint it.

When you play your maracas, the snakes will wriggle about and frighten everyone!

 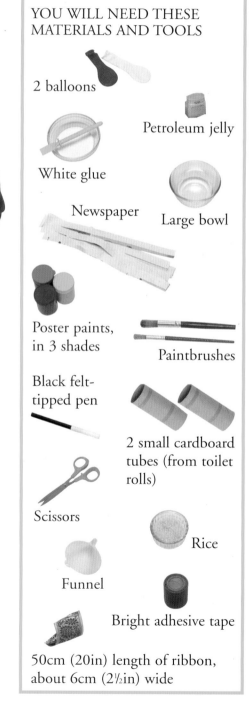

! Children may need help blowing up and tying the balloons, and with cutting the holes in the papier-mâché.

YOU WILL NEED THESE MATERIALS AND TOOLS

2 balloons

Petroleum jelly

White glue

Newspaper

Large bowl

Poster paints, in 3 shades

Paintbrushes

Black felt-tipped pen

2 small cardboard tubes (from toilet rolls)

Scissors

Rice

Funnel

Bright adhesive tape

50cm (20in) length of ribbon, about 6cm (2½in) wide

1 Blow up and tie the balloons. Cover them with petroleum jelly. Support the balloons in jars or mugs, otherwise they will bounce about.

2 Make up some paste using 3 parts glue to 1 part water. Tear the paper into strips and squares, then soak in the paste. Cover the balloons with the strips.

3 Leave to dry, then cover them with the squares. Wait for the second layer to dry, then paint the balloons. Leave the paint to dry.

4 Now paint the cardboard tubes, using a different shade. Leave the paint to dry.

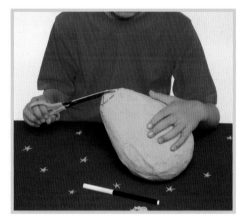

5 Draw around one of the cardboard tubes on the end of each balloon and cut out the circles.

6 Spread glue onto one end of each cardboard tube. Push them into the holes in the balloons for handles.

7 Pour the rice into the balloons through the handles. Seal the end of each handle with bright adhesive tape. Spread glue onto the handles, then cover them with ribbon.

8 Paint squiggly snakes to decorate the maracas. Use the black felt-tipped pen to draw the snakes' eyes and their forked tongues.

Making music

Shake both maracas together in time to the music. You can also play one maraca on its own. Hold it in one hand and roll it against the palm of your other hand.

Bottle Xylophone

Bottles make wonderful musical instruments. To get different notes out of them, you add more water. Play the xylophone with different sticks to make different sounds. You can also blow across the top of the bottles. Gabriella has put tinted water in her xylophone bottles. This looks pretty and it also helps her remember the different notes.

Making music

See if you can play a simple tune like "Three Blind Mice". Add a little water to each bottle or pour some out until you get the notes right.

! A grown-up should push the skewer into the cork. Never leave the dyed water in the bottles in case someone is tempted to try a taste. The water is NOT drinkable.

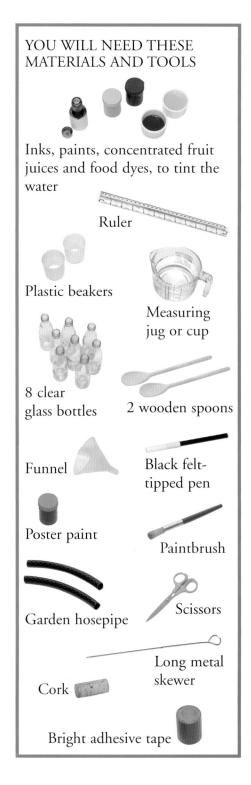

YOU WILL NEED THESE MATERIALS AND TOOLS

Inks, paints, concentrated fruit juices and food dyes, to tint the water

Ruler

Plastic beakers

Measuring jug or cup

8 clear glass bottles

2 wooden spoons

Funnel

Black felt-tipped pen

Poster paint

Paintbrush

Garden hosepipe

Scissors

Cork

Long metal skewer

Bright adhesive tape

1 Mix seven different shades of water. You could use inks, paints, food dyes and concentrated fruit juices.

2 Tap one of the empty glass bottles with a wooden spoon and listen to the sound it makes.

3 Using a black felt-tipped pen, mark 2cm (¾in) from the bottom of the bottle.

4 Pour one shade of water into the bottle up to the mark. This will be much easier if you use a funnel. Hit the bottle again – this time the sound will be slightly lower.

5 Pour a different shade of water into each bottle. Increase the level of the water by 2cm (¾in) each time. The bottle with the most water in it will give the lowest note.

6 Now try blowing across the top of each bottle. This time the bottle with the most water will give the highest note!

7 Paint the round ends of two wooden spoons. Cover the handles with hosepipe.

8 Make a different stick. Ask a grown-up to cut the cork in half and push in the skewer. Cover the cork with adhesive tape.

The different sticks make different sounds. What other sticks could you make or use?

Reed Pipe Man

Some instruments have a reed to help make the sound. A straw makes a good reed — instead of sucking, remember to blow through it! This pipe is a very simple kind of oboe and it makes quite a loud noise. Joshua has drawn a face on his pipe and given it a fancy, frilly collar.

Making music

Put the end of the straw in your mouth and grip it between your lips. Take a deep breath and blow *slowly*. You should sound just like a duck!

⚠️ Children may need help with scissors.

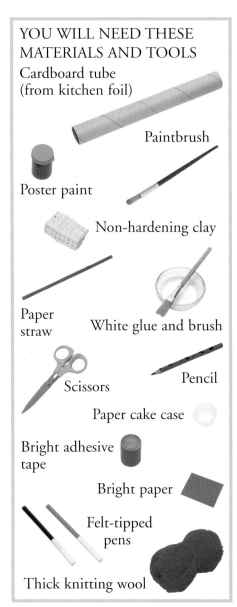

YOU WILL NEED THESE MATERIALS AND TOOLS

Cardboard tube (from kitchen foil)

Paintbrush

Poster paint

Non-hardening clay

Paper straw

White glue and brush

Scissors

Pencil

Paper cake case

Bright adhesive tape

Bright paper

Felt-tipped pens

Thick knitting wool

1 Paint the cardboard tube. Leave the paint to dry.

2 Press out a thick layer of clay. Push the end of the cardboard tube into the clay and cut out a circle.

3 Glue the clay circle into one end of the cardboard tube. Leave the glue to dry.

4 Cut the straw in half. Squash the end of one piece flat under a big book. Then snip off the corners of the flattened end. This will be the reed.

5 Make a hole in the middle of the clay using the pencil. Push the straw through the hole and pinch the clay around it.

6 Cut out the middle of the paper cake case. The frilly edge will make a very nice collar for your reed pipe man.

7 Cut the bright adhesive tape and paper into diamond shapes and use them to decorate the tube. Tape the cake-case collar around the tube about a third of the way down.

8 Draw a face on the tube, above the collar. Cut short pieces of wool and glue them on for the hair.

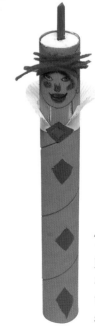

The reed pipe man is now ready to make some music!

Bugle Blow

The first bugles were used to send signals in battle or out hunting. Today bugles are used in the army, to wake everyone up in the morning! The soldier's bugle is a brass instrument but Claudius's bugle is made from a garden hosepipe.

! Children may need help cutting and positioning the hosepipe.

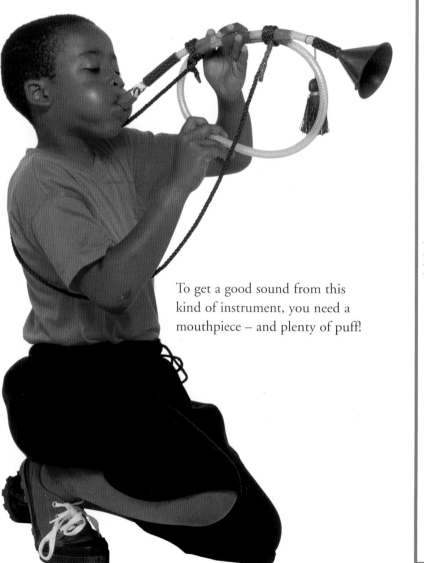

To get a good sound from this kind of instrument, you need a mouthpiece – and plenty of puff!

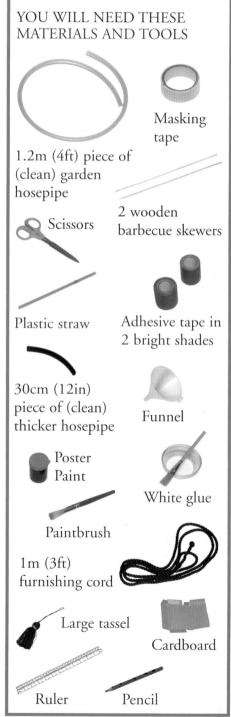

YOU WILL NEED THESE MATERIALS AND TOOLS

1.2m (4ft) piece of (clean) garden hosepipe

Masking tape

Scissors

2 wooden barbecue skewers

Plastic straw

Adhesive tape in 2 bright shades

30cm (12in) piece of (clean) thicker hosepipe

Funnel

Poster Paint

White glue

Paintbrush

1m (3ft) furnishing cord

Large tassel

Cardboard

Ruler

Pencil

1 Bend the thin hosepipe into a circle so that the ends overlap as shown. Bind the circle together with two pieces of masking tape 8cm (3in) apart.

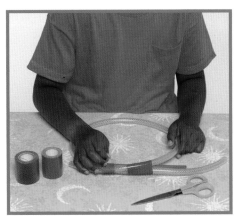

2 Push both skewers into the straw. Place the straw behind the join in the hosepipe and tape them together in three places.

3 Cut a piece of thick hosepipe about 15cm (6in) long. Slide it onto one end of the hosepipe. Cut a shorter length and slide it onto the other end.

4 Mix the poster paint with the same amount of glue and a little water, and then paint the funnel. Push the funnel into the longer piece of thick hosepipe.

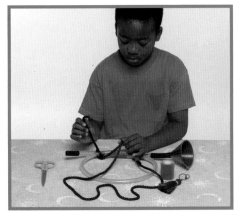

5 Tie the cord onto the bugle so that you can carry it across your chest. Fasten the tassel to the bugle.

6 Measure a square about 13 x 13cm (5 x 5in) on the cardboard and cut out using scissors.

7 Roll the square into a cone shape and trim. Tape the cone together and tape over the sharp cardboard edges.

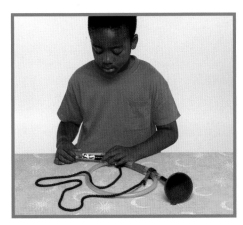

8 Fit the cone into the mouthpiece end of the bugle.

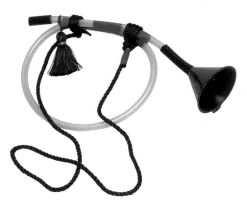

Making music

Rest the rim of the mouthpiece on your lips and take a deep breath. Buzz your lips into the mouthpiece. To play higher notes, blow faster.

Nail Chimes

You can make beautiful music with these nifty nail chimes. They are suspended from a cardboard tube and, because they hang freely, they make a lovely, clear, ringing sound when you strike them. You will need to find bolts in various sizes, so that your chimes will make different notes.

1 Cut a rectangle of paper as long as the cardboard tube and wide enough to fit around it. Stick the paper to the tube.

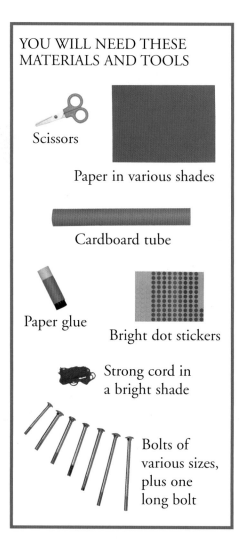

YOU WILL NEED THESE MATERIALS AND TOOLS

Scissors

Paper in various shades

Cardboard tube

Paper glue

Bright dot stickers

Strong cord in a bright shade

Bolts of various sizes, plus one long bolt

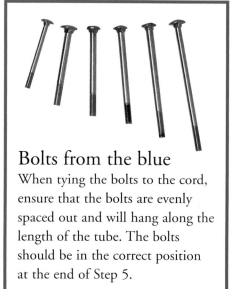

Bolts from the blue
When tying the bolts to the cord, ensure that the bolts are evenly spaced out and will hang along the length of the tube. The bolts should be in the correct position at the end of Step 5.

2 Put a neat row of bright dot stickers around each end of the cardboard tube, for decoration.

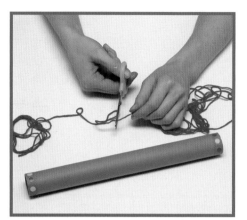

3 Cut a long length of strong cord, four times the length of the tube. It must be strong enough to bear the weight of all the bolts.

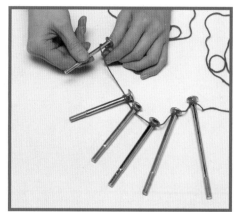

4 Ensure that you leave a length of cord twice as long as the tube free, then tie the heads of each bolt to the second quarter of the length of cord.

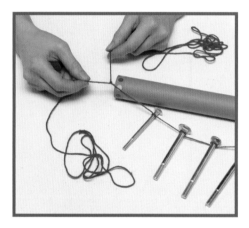

5 Thread the end of the cord that you left free through the tube. Tie it to the other piece of cord securely, to form a loop that goes through the tube, with a long trailing end.

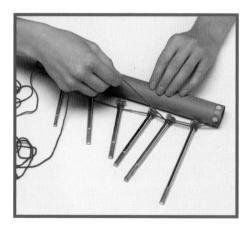

6 Loop the trailing cord two or three times around the head of each bolt again, then pass it back through the tube. Tie the ends tightly together.

Making music

Hold the tube with one hand and play the chimes using the long bolt with your other hand.

Flowerpot Chimes

These chimes sound very different from metal ones. Ilaira likes to play her chimes using wooden spoons, but you can also leave them to knock together gently in the wind. The best place to hang them is from a door frame or window frame. The flowerpots are very heavy, so you need a strong coathanger.

The finished flowerpot chimes, ready to play a tune. Ilaira has painted her spoons bright green.

Making music
Hit the flowerpots gently with the spoons. Does the small flowerpot sound different to the large one?

! A grown-up should make the holes in the corks and cut them in half with a craft knife. Children may need help with scissors.

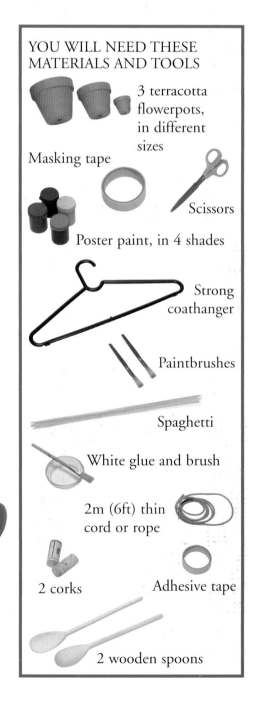

YOU WILL NEED THESE MATERIALS AND TOOLS

3 terracotta flowerpots, in different sizes

Masking tape

Scissors

Poster paint, in 4 shades

Strong coathanger

Paintbrushes

Spaghetti

White glue and brush

2m (6ft) thin cord or rope

2 corks

Adhesive tape

2 wooden spoons